Lost Dog Books, LLC
10000 Lakeshore Boulevard
Cleveland, OH 44108

ORDERING INFORMATION
This book is available for purchase in quantity

PRINTED IN THE UNITED STATES OF AMERICA

ISBN: 978-1-7349335-2-9
FIRST EDITION
25 24 23 22 21   10 9 8 7 6 5 4 3 2 1

Produced and designed by Randy Martin

martinDESIGN.info 38632

Contacts:

Leslie Yerkes | catalystconsultinggroupinc@gmail.com
Randy Martin | info@martindesign.info
Traci Harmon-Hay | traciharmonhay@gmail.com

Your FOREVER DOG

HOW IT FEELS WHEN SOMEONE LOVES YOU

Leslie Yerkes and Randy Martin

ILLUSTRATOR
Traci Harmon-Hay

Lost Dog BOOKS

Bratenahl OH

OTHER BOOKS

Leslie Yerkes
Fun Works: Creating Places Where People Love to Work
301 Ways to Have Fun at Work (WITH DAVE HEMSATH)
Beans: Four Principles for Running a Business in Good Times and Bad
(WITH CHARLES DECKER)
Beyond Kicks & Carrots: Motivation in the Twenty-First Century

Yerkes and Martin
They Just Don't Get it: Changing Resistance into Understanding
Lost Found and Forever: When You Make a Promise, Keep It.

Randy Martin
Wilbur: Son of the Big Bad Wolfe (WITH ROSEMARIE LEMIEUX)
Sebastian Calls 911: Teaching Little-Ones How to Call for Help in an Emergency
(WITH JONI NOWAK)
Tale of the Nite-Kite: When You Believe, Magic Happens
(WITH JONI NOWAK)

Tracy Harmon-Hay
Speaking Frenchie
Chicken Dreams
Child's Fortune

To those who choose kindness and compassion
towards all animals and people.

Thank you to all who foster, fund, and rescue animals.

And to those who helped with the rescue of Big Boy
and supported his successful assimilation into our family.

I HAVE HIDDEN IN THESE BUSHES
FOR A LONG TIME.

When it got light enough to see, I would hide.
When it was dark and hard to see, I'd walk all around this field,
trying to find things to eat.
And water to drink.

There wasn't very much and I was always hungry.
And unless it rained, I'd be thirsty, too.

But I was safe. And that man couldn't hurt me anymore.
It was my choice to be hungry instead of being hurt.

EVEN IN THE DARK, I COULD HEAR PEOPLE.

And cars. And of course, the trains that moved every
night, in and out of the space next to where I lived.

BUT I STAYED AWAY FROM THEM.

I didn't think it was safe.
Safe is good.

ONE DAY, THOUGH, IT CHANGED.

It was light out and I was in my bushes, but I was awake.
I was waiting and watching.

The day before, right before the dark happened,
a human came into my space with a dog. A very big dog.

The human wasn't a man, I know that.
Is this what they call a woman?

WHEN THE WOMAN WALKED INTO MY FIELD, SHE SAW ME.

She sat down with her dog next to her.
They were both looking at me.
And she had food. I could smell it.
It was the best smell I'd ever smelled.

I wanted to sneak up and grab it right away.
But being safe is more important to me than food.
So I laid down on my stomach and waited to see if she might
forget some food when she left.
Then she called to me:

*"Big Boy. You really are a big boy.
Do you want some chicken?"*

I DIDN'T KNOW THEN WHAT CHICKEN WAS.

I thought if that was what smelled so good,
I wanted to taste it.
But I was still afraid. Afraid she might hit me,
like that man used to do before he left me here.
But I was really hungry.
So I decided to take a chance
and see if I could get closer to her.
I knew if I needed to get away,
I could run faster than she could.
She only had two legs. How fast could she be?

I STARTED TO CRAWL SLOWLY,
with my empty belly sliding along the ground.

She called to me.
But not as loud as that chicken was calling.

When I got about two dog spaces away from her,
I just couldn't make myself get any closer.
So I stopped and looked.
I think I must have been drooling because she did something
strange. She put the chicken on the ground and both she
and her dog backed away another two dog spaces.

THE CHICKEN SMELLED SO GOOD,
I COULDNT HELP MYSELF.
I leaped up, grabbed it, and ran back to my bushes
where I gobbled it down so fast, my belly began to hurt.
But I decided it was a good hurt. Then she called again.

"We'll see you tomorrow with more food."

She said she would be back every day. And feed me until I
trusted her enough to come home with her. And be safe.
She promised. Then she said,

"You're a big boy but you need someone to love you."

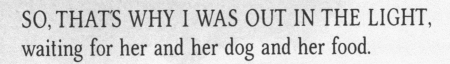

SO, THAT'S WHY I WAS OUT IN THE LIGHT,
waiting for her and her dog and her food.

I hoped she'd have some more chicken.
Yum.

I wasn't really sure she wouldn't hit me. I hoped not.
There was so much about humans I didn't know.
But I could already smell that chicken.

"Today, we're going to feast on canned dog food,"
she told me.

She said it wasn't chicken, but it was good.

And that her dog, Buddha Bear, really liked it.

"Let's see what you think," she said.

I DECIDED TO TAKE ANOTHER CHANCE.

So, I walked slowly toward her and her dog, Buddha Bear.
When I got to two dog spaces, I took a deep breath
and then took one more step closer.

As I did, she took out this shiny stick
with a round end on it, stuck it in the can,
and gave some food to her dog.

Buddha Bear gobbled it down.
Was she going to give some to me?

"Here you go, Big Boy, it's your turn."

I WAS MORE THAN HAPPY TO SHARE THE FOOD
WITH BUDDHA BEAR.

It was some of the best food I'd ever tasted.

When the can was empty, she opened another one
and we traded bites until that can was empty, too.

The food filled my belly. My tail moved fast — back and forth.
I felt good standing next to her dog — sharing.

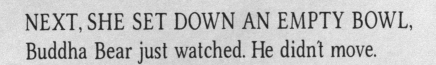

NEXT, SHE SET DOWN AN EMPTY BOWL,
Buddha Bear just watched. He didn't move.

Then she took out a bottle and twisted it
and poured WATER into the bowl!
Where did that come from?

Buddha Bear stepped forward and took a drink.
Then he stepped back and looked at me.
Like he was telling me it was my turn.
So I sighed again, stepped to the bowl,
and drank every last drop.

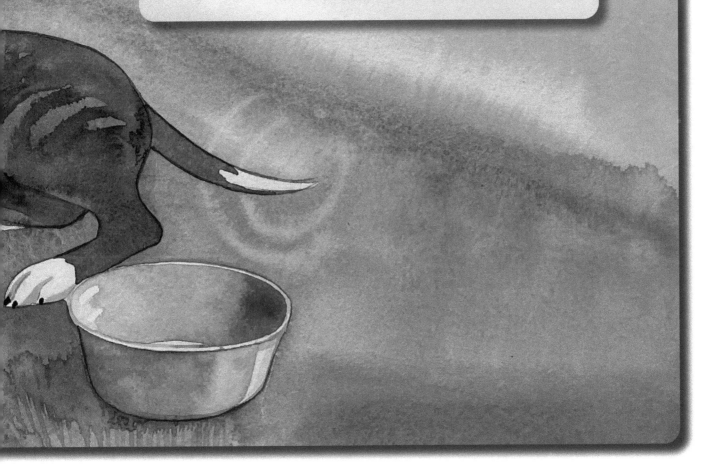

"You must have been thirsty, Big Boy."

She said she was sorry there was only one bottle.
But she promised us that the next time
she would bring two.

Then she packed up the bowl and the empty bottle
and she and Buddha Bear headed toward the gate.

"We'll be back tomorrow, Big Boy. See you then."

AS THEY WALKED TOWARD THE GATE,
I WALKED SLOWLY BEHIND.

When I got to the gate, I thought about going with them.
But I didn't.
I turned back toward my bushes
and decided it was time for a nap.

The truth was, I was too scared to go.

And that's how it went for many, many days.

I STARTED TO WATCH FOR THE WOMAN
AND BUDDHA BEAR EVERY DAY.

The people who worked in the factory
started to notice because I was out in the light.

They would set down food for me,
but I wouldn't get close to them like I did to her.

ONE TIME, SHE BROUGHT A BLANKET.

It smelled like her and her dog. She gave it to me.
I really liked it and walked all around with it in my mouth.

When they went home, I had their smell in my blanket
and I would sleep with it every time it got dark
and bring it out to show them when they came in the light.

The days were getting colder and the light was getting shorter.
So the dark was longer, too.

THEN ONE DAY, ANOTHER WOMAN CAME
WITH SOME MEN.

And they had sticks with ropes on them and sticks
with nets. They talked nice and slow like the woman
and her dog, but then they started to chase me
and wave those sticks at me.

But since I'd been eating her food, I was strong
and I ran away from them almost all of the light time.
Then they gave up and left. I was afraid again.
Did that woman send them to catch me?

JUST BEFORE THE DARK CAME,
THAT WOMAN AND HER DOG SHOWED UP.

I would only stick my head out of the bushes when she called.
She walked closer and wasn't smiling, like she always did.
And Buddha Bear was acting strange.

I think he was sad.

SHE SAT DOWN, RIGHT IN THE FIELD.

Buddha Bear put his head in her lap
and they both looked at me.
I think they were crying.

I felt sad for her and walked slowly up them.
Then, I put my head in her lap, too, and she petted my head.
Buddha Bear lifted up his head and nuzzled me.

23

EVEN THOUGH I HAD JUST BEEN CHASED
by people with sticks, I felt comfortable with
them both.

I felt good when I was around them.

SHE SAT WITH ME, SANG TO ME,

I liked her. And Buddha Bear, too.
And I liked that my tummy was full.
I wondered if this was what it felt like
when someone loves you.

25

I KNEW I WANTED TO BE WITH THEM.

And that I wanted this family thing she always talked about.
But sometimes my bones still ached where that man had hit me.
It wasn't easy to forget what it felt like to be hit.
And I still wasn't sure I could trust humans.

But, this felt good. It felt right.
I got up and walked back to my bushes.

They left to go home through the gate.
This time, I was certain the woman was crying.
I wasn't sure about Buddha Bear. But he probably was, too.

THE WOMAN AND BUDDHA BEAR
KEPT SHOWING UP WITH FOOD.

I kept eating it and sharing it with Buddha Bear.
Buddha Bear and I would do a lot of running around.
He told me we were playing. I liked him. And I liked her.
She filled my bowls with food and water and I would eat.
Then I would stand next to her.
This time she put her hand down on my head.
I liked that. Then, she put something around my neck.
She called it a collar and I realized I didn't mind. I sighed.
I thought about running but I didn't.

WHEN I WAS DONE EATING SHE PUT A PIECE OF
ROPE ON THE COLLAR AROUND MY NECK.

And the three of us walked out the gate.
I saw that Buddha Bear had on a collar with that leash thing
hooked on. Just like me. And I realized Buddha Bear had
ALWAYS had them. I just didn't notice because they weren't
mean or nasty. They were just the way a dog and human show
love and respect for each other.

So, I thought I'd be fine doing that, too.

AS I WALKED BEHIND HER AND BUDDHA BEAR
WALKED IN FRONT, SHE STARTED SINGING.

Slowly, we walked down the street.
I was leaving my field and my home. And you know what?
I was just fine with that because I knew I would be safe.

And loved.

29

THERE'S A NICE YARD WHERE I LIVE NOW,
WHERE BOTH BUDDHA BEAR AND I LIVE.

And a pile of toys outside and a house to go inside when
it rains, snows, or is too cold or too hot to be outside.

OUR WATER BOWLS ARE ALWAYS FULL.

I check them all the time, just to be sure I'm still loved.

We get fed two times a day and I'm never hungry.
Sometimes, when she is "training" me, I get treats.
I love to learn!

SHE LOVES TO CUDDLE AND KISS.

I like to share the warmth of their bed
and snuggle with Buddha Bear.
I really like having a brother.

The woman is great, but she can't run with me
like Buddha Bear can.
But he can't feed me.
So we're each special in our own way.

SOMETIMES, I STILL HAVE BAD DREAMS.

About the man and the field.
And all the cold and hunger I used to have.

But when I do, she's always there to make me feel better.

Buddha Bear does that, too.

EVERY DAY, WE WALK
next to the biggest puddle
I could ever imagine.

I can't even see the other side!

WHEN I'M OUT IN THE YARD,
I use my voice to let people know I'm here.

My little nub of a tail moves fast when she's around.
I wonder if this is what it's supposed to be like
when you're in a family.

35

EVERYBODY CALLS ME BIG BOY.

I feel strong and healthy.
I am not hungry or cold.

Now it's my turn to make a promise.

I WILL BE YOUR FOREVER DOG.

I will love you and protect you.

I will be your family, too.

Thank you for your promise to me.

And . . .

FOR CHOOSING ME TO LOVE.

WOOF!

EPILOGUE

After two months of learning to trust, Big Boy joined his first, and only family. There he learned the ways of the human world as well as the language and etiquette of being a dog. He was a fast learner, bright, and eager to please.

Big Boy was 150 pounds of enthusiasm and love who taught his human family that trust can be recovered, love restored, and hearts healed. Every day he learned something new and showed delight in the simplest things.

He brightened lives and complicated them at the same time.

Big Boy wasn't just rescued, he rescued back. He was a professor of compassion and an instructor in opening hearts. His lessons of love gave rise to the rescue of another dog and a cat, as well as a senior mother from a situation that did not reflect her definition of quality of life.

Everyone who ever met Big Boy loved him and was loved back. He was the living and loving poster dog for how it feels when someone loves you.

BIOGRAPHIES

LESLIE YERKES

Leslie Yerkes is an organizational development/change management consultant in Cleveland, Ohio. She founded Catalyst Consulting Group, Inc. in 1987 with a simple philosophy: People are basically good, well-intentioned, courageous, and able to learn. Her job is to provide a framework in which people can draw on their own inner resources to find creative solutions.

A cum laude graduate of Wittenberg University, Leslie earned her Master of Science in Organizational Development from Case Western Reserve University. She has taught at John Carroll University, Baldwin Wallace College, The Mandel School of Applied Social Science, and is on the faculty at the Weatherhead Dively Center for Executive Education.

Her business goal is to help people create sustainable organizations. Her life goal is to create the framework in which people can draw on their own resources to find creative solutions. A measure of Leslie's success as a business leader and consultant is that she first applies to herself the principles in which she engages her clients. Her clients have included Chrysler Corporation, The Cleveland Clinic Foundation, Lake Hospital System, The United Church of America, Westfield Companies, and Mittal Steel USA. A sub specialty of Leslie's is making non-profits healthy and sustainable.

Leslie is the author of six previous books that have been translated into more than a dozen languages and have sold hundreds of thousands of copies worldwide.

You can visit Leslie's website at www.leslieyerkes.com

RANDY MARTIN

Randy Martin began his career as a television producer-director-writer. Following that, he owned an advertising agency specializing in marketing supermarkets and was the creator, editor, and publisher of "In The Neighborhood," a local tabloid newspaper that promoted supermarkets and the communities in which they resided.

Eventually his passion turned to books and the web. He is a graphic designer, ghost writer, editor (seven books), and book designer with seven MarCom Awards, two Summit Awards, two Ippy Awards, and one Mom's Choice Award to his credit. He also has two MarCom awards for web design and a dozen Emmys as a television producer/director/writer. He was the director of the Cleveland Browns' "Masters of the Gridiron" (YouTube).

This is his third co-authoring project with Leslie Yerkes. The two have 4 more books in the works, with several more in the talking stages.

He serves on the board of directors for the Desoto Arts Council, The Hernando Veteran's Parade, and the Friends of the Von Theatre. In his spare time, he sings and plays guitar with Mississippi Greystone.

Randy is the owner of martinDESIGN.info

TRACI HARMON-HAY

Traci Harmon-Hay received her BFA in illustration and painting from the Maryland Institute Collage of Art (MICA). Represented by New York's Creative Freelancers, Harmon-Hay co-founded Studio Six, an illustration co-op in Baltimore MD. Her clients included the *Washington Times, Baltimore Sun, Nation's Business Magazine*, Yankee Publishing, and the *Provincetown Independent*.

Traci is the founder of the Harmon Gallery in Wellfleet. She has also exhibited her work at the Left Bank Gallery, Fountain Street Gallery, Bromfield Gallery, Cotuit Center for the Arts, Cahoon Museum, and Cape Cod Museum of Art. She teaches art privately and at the Provincetown Art Association and Museum.

Traci has also written and illustrated:

Speaking Frenchie
Chicken Dreams
Child's Fortune

Traci lives in Wellfleet, MA with her husband and two daughters. You can visit Traci's website at www.traciharmonhay.com

TO ORDER BOOKS AND READ MORE ABOUT BIG BOY
AND HIS FAMILY GO TO:
HTTPS://WWW.LOSTDOGBOOKS.COM

Bratenahl OH

CPSIA information can be obtained
at www.ICGtesting.com
Printed in the USA
LVHW051606031221
704784LV00002B/6